classical masterpieces for cello

Table Of Contents

Bach 1

Six Cello Suites 1 2

Six Cello Suites 2 7

Six Cello Suites 3 11

Six Cello Suites 4 17

Six Cello Suites 5 24

Six Cello Suites 6 30

Chopin 38

Nocturne 39

Vivaldi 41

Allegro 42

Sonata 44

Winter 47

Pachelbel 48

Canon In D 49

Elgar 50

Concerto 51

Bruch 54

Kol Nidrei 55

Beethoven 57

Sonata 58

Sonatina 62

Ode To Joy 63

W.H Squire 64

Serenade 65

Tarantella 67

Tchaikovsky 71

Swan Lake Theme 72

Valse Sentimentale 73

Johann Sebastian Bach
German Composer, 1685-1750

Six Cello Suites
No. 1 in G major, BWV 1007

Johann Sebastian Bach

Six Cello Suites
No. 2 in D minor, BWV 1008

Johann Sebastian Bach

Prélude

Six Cello Suites
No. 3 in C major, BWV 1009

Johann Sebastian Bach

Six Cello Suites
No. 4 in E♭ major, BWV 1010

Johann Sebastian Bach

Six Cello Suites
No. 5 in C minor, BWV 1011

Johann Sebastian Bach

Allemande

Courante

Six Cello Suites
No. 6 in C minor, BWV 1012

Johann Sebastian Bach

Gigue

Frédéric Chopin
Polish Composer, 1810-1849

Nocturne Op. 9 No. 2

Frederic Chopin

Antonio Vivaldi
Italian Composer, 1678-1741

Allegro From Concerto In D Major

Antonio Vivaldi

Sonata No. 5

Antonio Vivaldi

Winter

Antonio Vivaldi

Johann Pachelbel

German Composer, 1653-1706

Canon In D

Johann Pachelbel

Edward Elgar
English Composer, 1857-1934

Concerto From Op. 85

Edward Elgar

Max Bruch

German Composer, 1838-1920

Kol Nidrei

Max Bruch

Ludwig van Beethoven
German Composer, 1770-1827

Sonata No. 5 In F Major, Op. 24

Ludwig Van Beethoven

Sonatina

Ludwig Van Beethoven

Ode To Joy

Ludwig van Beethoven

William Henry Squire
British Composer, 1871-1963

Sérénade

William Henry Squire

Tarantella

William Henry Squire

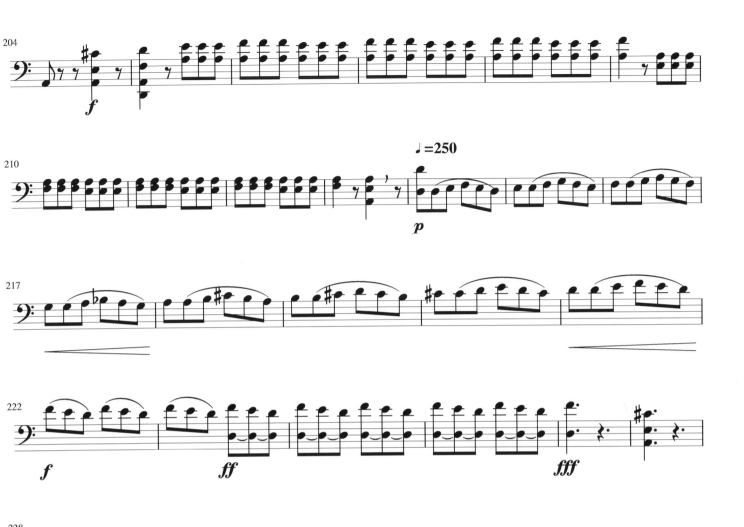

Pyotr Ilyich Tchaikovsky
Russian Composer, 1840-1893

Swan Lake Theme

Pyotr Ilyich Tchaikovsky

Valse Sentimentale Op. 51 No. 6

Pyotr Ilyich Tchaikovsky

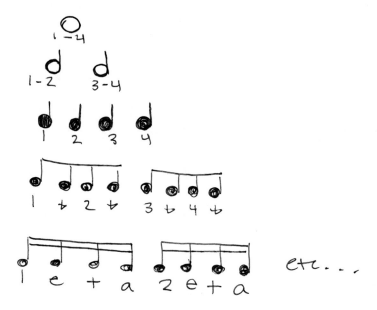

Made in the USA
Columbia, SC
09 January 2024